Thomas Vaughan

Morah

The Indian Wife

Thomas Vaughan

Morah
The Indian Wife

ISBN/EAN: 9783744776615

Printed in Europe, USA, Canada, Australia, Japan

Cover: Foto ©Thomas Meinert / pixelio.de

More available books at **www.hansebooks.com**

MORAH;

OR,

THE INDIAN WIFE;

A Moral Tale:

ALSO,

SONGS AND BALLADS;

AND

THE APPARITION; A TALE OF HEREFORD,

FOUNDED UPON FACT.

BY THE LATE THOMAS VAUGHAN.

HEREFORD:

PRINTED BY EDWARD WYMSS, AND SOLD BY ALL BOOKSELLERS.

1863.

TO

MRS. LOUISA WILSON,

OF THE HALL-NOOK,

PENKETH, NEAR WARRINGTON, LANCASHIRE,

THE PRESENT VOLUME IS GRATEFULLY AND RESPECTFULLY DEDICATED, IN CONFORMITY WITH THE WISHES OF THE LAMENTED AUTHOR.

━━━━━━━━━━━━━━━

It will be seen from the terms of the above Dedication, that Thomas Vaughan, the "Tailor Poet," is no more—he died in the Hereford Infirmary on Tuesday night, October 27, 1863, at the age of 50 years, and was interred on Sunday the 1st instant, in Saint Owen's Burial-ground, a large number of sorrowing friends attending the funeral.

The death of the Author, whose last production is now presented to the public in the hope of serving his surviving children, was tranquil. His attenuated frame and anxious mind, worn out with the battle of this life, yielded calmly to the decree which transferred him to another. May we not reasonably hope that the change has been a gain to him? His wife—the solace, comfort, and effectual support in all his trials, died some few years ago, and thus with her he finds a peaceful asylum, different indeed to that alluded to in our Introductory Notice, but not the less sheltered from the storms and trials of adversity.

It remains only to be stated that the present volume would have appeared several weeks ago, but that the Author wished to add to its contents, when he was attacked by the illness which prevented him from doing so, although he had a strong expectation that he should recover. The proof-sheets were corrected by Mr. Vaughan, but some few typographical blunders have crept in, for which the indulgence of the reader is solicited.

Nov. 5, 1863.

INTRODUCTORY REMARKS.

BY A FRIEND.

I⊤ is observed by the sweetest and most elegant of our pastoral bards, that in a rude state of society poetry is an object of cultivation ;—judging by what is passing around us, the converse of this appears to prevail at the present day : in an advanced condition of civilization the love of poetry declines ; or rather, we should say, becomes perverted. How otherwise can we account for the recent fact of a numerous body of noblemen, gentlemen, and tradesmen signing a Memorial to the Chief Minister of the Crown in favour of one whose effusions do not rise above the level of those of Grub-street or the Seven Dials—nay worse, whose lucubrations are disfigured by gross personalities ? If a proper interest were taken in the productions of the Muse, should we have seen the better classes of the land recommending *such* a poet as a suitable recipient of the royal bounty on account of the excellence of his verses ! or a prime minister endorsing that opinion by ranking him " in the same category as Burns ! " O thou sweet bard of Scotia, fair mountain child of Genius and native Mirth, how art thou shamed by such a comparison ! Had something been done by the state for Mr. THOS. VAUGHAN, of Hereford, every one who has perused his writings or is acquainted with his character. would have in-

B

stantly felt that a service, sorely required, had been done to a man of worth and talent.

The feeling that nothing *permanent* has yet been done for our local bard, has elicited the foregoing remarks ; yet now once again he comes before the public with an Offering which it is earnestly hoped will prove generally acceptable. The Tale of the " Indian Wife " carries with it a moral deserving of all acceptation. What is it but a faithful portrait in verse of a scene too frequent in this busy world of ours—Affection, Honour, Reason itself, all sacrificed to the Moloch of Drink ! His Minor Poems speak for themselves ; and of the whole volume, although, doubtless, it may be said that there are little inelegancies—(for our poet does not profess to have received a learned education,) still, the ever-memorable and just criticism of Horace is to be borne in mind :

" —— ubi plura nitent in carmine, non ego paucis
" Offendar maculis."——

If our poet has not attained the summit of Parnassus, he has culled many flowers by the way, and arranged them in a graceful bouquet worthy of the acceptance of the fair and the candid.

The remarkable incident narrated in the Prose Tale which forms the sequel to the present volume, is suggestive of curious reflection. The writer of the present notice well remembers the sensation occasioned by the visit of the " resurrectionists " to this city ; and the term " Burkers' Cottage," applied to their temporary docile, is probably not yet forgotten. Without, however, hazarding an opinion as to the cause of the apparition, it may be remarked that however a prelate and others may toil in testing things supernatural by human reason, the great Observer of human nature (Shakspere) was right when he said that there are more things in the sky and on the earth than are dreamt of in philosophy.

The two reflections arising out of the Narration are these—Do disembodied spirits return to earth in visible form? and can imaginary objects be so imprinted upon the retina as to be clearly discernible by some, whilst they have no existence to others? This indeed does not admit of doubt, as a singular case which shall be given, adds another proof to many others : in the present instance, indeed, the mystery is, that three individuals in a position for calm observation, were affected at the same time—hence we are thrown back on the more solemn reflection, upon which point let us quote the sentiment of a man of the highest intellect, of strict morality, and sterling piety. Dr. Johnson has the following passages in his beautiful Tale of *Rasselas* :—

" If all your fear be of apparitions," said the prince, " I will promise you safety : there is no danger from the dead : he that is once buried will be seen no more."

" That the dead are seen no more," said Imlac, " I will not undertake to maintain against the concurrent and unvaried testimony of all ages, and of all nations. There is no people, rude or learned, among whom apparitions of the dead are not related and believed. This opinion, which, perhaps, prevails as far as human nature is diffused, could become universal only by its truth : those that never heard of one another, would not have agreed in a tale which nothing but experience can make credible. That it is doubted by single cavillers, can very little weaken the general evidence, and some who deny it with their tongues, confess it by their fears."

The case of spectral illusion, to which reference was made, occurred to Mr. Hone, the very clever Compiler of the *Every-day Book*, and was as follows :—

" In 1823, the Editor being mentally disordered from too close application, left home in the afternoon to consult a medical friend, and obtain relief under his extreme depression. In Fleet-street, on the opposite side of the way to where he was walking, he saw a pair of legs devoid of body, which he was persuaded were his own legs, though not at all like them. A few days afterwards, when worse in health, he went to the same friend for a similar purpose, and on his way saw himself on precisely the same spot as he had imagined he had seen his legs, but with this difference, that the person was entire, and thoroughly a likeness as to feature, form, and dress. The appearance seemed as real as his own existence."

And now a concluding word for the Author. This is not a mere appeal *ad misericordiam*—to the charity of the public; yet what forbids a friend from placing the facts before the reader? The poet. labouring under " want and disease. fell pair."—with bodily infirmities that prevent him from pursuing his trade—eye-sight failing, and the sweet harmonies of nature for ever shut out from him by the privation of the sense of hearing, needs assistance. In the first place this can be essentially done by the purchase of his book. There is a noble band of Ministers of the Gospel who, witnessing the sin and folly of intemperance, are, by way of example, abstaining altogether from the " accursed thing ;"—how could they better serve the excellent cause which they have undertaken, than by placing upon the table of every reading-room this Tale of " Morah," which depicts the consequences of the soul and body-destroying vice? Still further: a boon indeed would it be if those gentlemen who are the managers of public institutions established for the solace of cases such as this, would grant him an asylum in which he might pass the remainder of his days in tranquillity, and justify the appointment by the grateful propriety of his conduct. Failing these hopes and means. one course alone is left to him---a resort to his parochial settlement.

THE INDIAN WIFE.

CANTO I.

" A thousand evil beings there are, that hate
" To look on happiness ;—these hurt, impede,
" And, leagued with time, circumstance, and fate,
" Keep kindred heart from heart, to pine, and pant, and bleed."

BROOKS.

'Twas morning, and a fair spring sun
Had 'gan his daily course to run ;
Already had he lightly tipped
The hill tops, and had softly sipped
The sparkling dew, that trembling hung
The teeming shrubs and plants among ;
All, all was glad and blithesome there ;
The prowling wolf had sought his lair ;
The savage panther, too, had crept
To where her cubs in darkness slept,
And left the scene to others now,
Who sprang aloft from every bough ;
The feathered tribe and busy bee
Now sang and hummed on bush and tree.
 And other dwellers now were seen
To enter on that charming scene ;—
Man—enterprising, thrifty man,
His work of husbandry began :
For in that far-off, lonely place,
Where late alone the Red-man's face
Was seen, the White-man's huts now stood ;
Some twenty of them flanked the wood,
Which stretched afar, as though to note
The broad dark line by Nature wrote,

To mark the bound'ry of each race
That owned a different-coloured face.
    One hut was there that seemed to shun
The rest ;—a gloomy-looking one
It was : its aspect seemed to mark
It as a place where any dark
Or knavish deed might there be done,
As safe as elsewhere 'neath the sun.
It was, ostensibly, a *store*,
Where whiskey, rum, and many more
Such like things were to be had,—
" To ease the sick, or cheer the sad ! "
So said its host, Elnathan Slack,
And none were there who dared attack
The character of House or Host,
For there all civil laws were lost ;
And " might was right ;" and Slack being *strong*,
Was very seldom in the wrong.
    No patch of cultivated ground,
Nor meadow-land, was seen around
That lone, suspicious-looking hut ;
And yet Elnathan Slack could put
His hand upon more property
Than of his neighbours any three !
How he got it will be shown
Within my tale, as I go on.
    Well,—on the morning of my tale
Our Yankee host sat on the rail
That stretched across his cabin front,
And bent beneath the load upon't :—
Slack stood six feet in " stocking feet,"
And his great limbs were firmly set ;
His shoulders round, and on his head
Flourished rough locks of *sandy* red.

And there he sat,—a listless, lazy
Lump of nature;—many days he
Spent in no one occupation,
Save his present situation
On " the rail."—He'd not sat there
Long, on that same morning, ere
His practised ear caught up the sound
Of horse's hoofs upon the ground.
He turned to whence they came, and saw
(Beneath his broad and bony paw
Spread o'er his eyes), a horse and man,
And knowing both, he thus began :
    " What, Redskin ! wall, now, darn my shirt,
If you red chaps, now, aint no dirt
At airly risin !—for, I'll pound,
You must have rid five miles of ground
This blessed mornin, at a breath,
To come here jist to wash yer teeth !
I said last night I know'd yer'd come
To git another snack o' rum."
    The Indian stopped before the door :
His fine but fevered features bore
The marks of late and deep excess,
That proved his inward wretchedness !
He slid from off his panting beast,
And thus the wily host addressed :
    " My pale-faced friend will give me more
Of fire-water from his store ?
My heart is low, my temples beat,
My throat is sore with burning heat,
Like to our prairie hunting plain,
When cracks the ground for want of rain."
    " Give !" cried the White-man ; " if I give,
Why, how am I myself to live ?

I cannot give, but I will sell,
Or dicker* with ye, if yer will."
   "Sell !" cried the savage ; "gold I've none
To purchase with---all mine is gone ;
My peltries, too, now swell thy store,
And birds may safely round me soar ;
The wolf may follow on my trail,
The buff 'lo heedless snuff the gale ;
I now must from the panther flee,
Though once the monster fled from me ;
No more by me the bears are shot,---
Thou hast my faithful rifle got !
I cannot e'en the beavers snare ;---
Are they more cunning than they were ?
Not so ! 'tis I am grown more dull ?
The dams with beaver still are full,
But fly me not ;---they seem to know
I have no traps to catch them now."
   His eye rolled, with a meaning glare,
Upon his host, but found not there
One pitying glance to meet his look ;---
So moaned he, till his fine frame shook ;
But not with passion,---that was dead,
And all his nobler feelings fled :
His head sank listless on his breast,
His arms were folded o'er his chest :
I have him now within my eye,
The picture of despondency.
   "Where are," he cried, and fixed his stare
Upon the calm and vacant air ;
"My steady hand, my watchful sight,
That once could trace the eagle's flight ?

---

* Barter, or exchange,

My deer-like bound? All, all are gone !
Thy drink hath made me old too soon."
He paused again to catch each thought
Reflection to his memory brought ;---
He pondered o'er the happy time
Ere white men breathed his native clime ;
He viewed himself as he was, when
But yet a boy, he sat with men,
And listened at the council-fire
To deeds that made his soul aspire
To emulate them.   Next he thought
When foremost of his band he fought,
And twenty scalp-locks graced his knee
As trophies of his victory !
Regretful memory wandered back
To times when he would dare attack
The gaunt wolf or the shaggy bear,
And boldly face them in their lair !
He saw himself, his horse and hound,
As erst he swept the hunting ground,
Proud ! dauntless ! bravest of the brave !
When bowed his heart to no one,---save
Her, whose heart had bowed to none,
Until by him its price was won.
    It was in fight, where he had saved
His chief, her sire, who there had braved
A host of foes, who did surround,
And beat the aged chief to ground ;
When he, with hatchet dropping blood,
As quick as thought his chief bestrode,
And dealt about him blows that fell
Resistless !—each one rang a knell
Of death ; yet paused he not to deck,
With spoil of foes, his knee or neck ;

C

But dragged his chief with gentle force,
And scathless placed him on his horse,
Just as the yell of triumph rose
Above their fell and fallen foes,
Who, vanquished, were compelled to yield,
And leave them masters of the field.

    Such was the deed by which he won
The high-souled Morah as his own.

    He thought of this ;—remembered more ;—
Knew, oh ! how blessed he was, before
He e'er had touched the curse of man ;
Then all his miseries began !
Till then his heart was bravely gay,
His head clear as a sunny day ;
No cares perplexed his even mind,
His acts untrammelled as the wind ;
His days in healthful pleasures went,
His nights in gentle sleep were spent ;
His brow reclining on *her* breast
Upon whose faithful heart he'd rest ;---
That heart which beat for him alone,---
That heart which *once had been* his own !
But that was time gone past ;---at least
She loved the man, *but not the beast !*
She loved him while he loved his home,
Or with his kindred loved to roam :
Oh then, at early blush of morn,
With pride she would her lord adorn ;—
Would deck him for the war or chase,
And yield the parting, fond embrace.

    And then at eve,---sweet balmy eve,
Her lonely wigwam would she leave,
And quick ascend the neighbouring brow
To scan the spreading plains below :

And there she'd watch, despite the hour,
Which left her wholly at the power
Of hostile bands, or beasts of prey,
Which leave their haunts at close of day ;---
She'd watch for him, and when he came,
Discomfited, or crowned with fame,
'Twas one to her ; she soothed his grief,
Or shared the triumphs of her chief :
Would hang with rapture on his neck,
And look the joy she could not speak.
But now this bliss had left his arms,---
Wife, wigwam,---all had lost their charms!
What wonder, then, that he should sigh,
While thinking of the misery
His faults had brought upon his head,
And made him far, far worse than dead ?---
What wonder that his heart should sink
Within him, should he dare to think ?
And think he must till steeped in drink.
    " The cup! the dram!" he wildly cried,
" In which I from myself may hide!
Oh! give it me, that I may sink
These bitter thoughts deep, deep in drink!
Release me from this mental chain,
And let my spirit soar again!
'Tis thou canst do it,---aye, in sooth,
'Tis thou canst give me back---my youth."

    The cunning Yankee met the eye
That bent upon him eagerly,
As half in hope, and half in dread,
It watched him, till at length he said.
" Why look you here, now, 'tarnal death!
What need is thar to waste your breath ?

I guess you thinks I stole my rum,
And that my gin as slickly come;
And that I must have come out west
To *give* the Redskins all a feast!
I reckon, if I have yer traps,
You've had their worth, lad, in your chops.
But I aint hard---jist reason talk,
And see if I yer fancy baulk.
I've bin your friend,---I am so still.
And shall hang on so, if ye will:
Jist try me on in any way,
Aud call me " skunk " if I say nay.
　　And here I am ! Elnathan Slack,
Can break an alligator's back ;
Can lick a panther in a trice,
Or hug a bear,---for I aint nice !
Aye ! when my dander's up, I'll take
The jacket off a rattle-snake ;
And if at that the brute should rail,
I'll make the varmint eat his tail !
I'll crack a tortoise like a flea,
And grin the bark clean off a tree ;
Or if it should my humour suit,
I'll cuss the tree up by the root.
Yet I aint savage now, I'll own,
But timid as a hunted 'coon ;
And wish to keep so, to the full ;
But---dont you stroke me 'ginst the wool."
　　The Indian cowed beneath his glance,
And stood awhile as in a trance ;
His faculties all prostrate laid,
'Numbed for a time : at length he said,
" I called thee brother,---thought thee one,
But now my worldly wealth is gone,

You show me 1 myself may go !
Do brothers serve each other so ?
The time hath been you claimed a kin
To me, in heart, though not in skin :
Our hearts were brothers, saidst thou not,
As oft we in thy wigwam sat ?
If thou didst take the name in vain,
And speak the thing thou didst not mean,
The serpent tribe to thee belongs,
As they, like thee, have got two tongues !
And since it is so, here we part ;—
I go, but with a heavy heart,
Since, for the first time, now I find
'Tis to *thyself* thou hast been kind ;
And as thou dost deny my suit,
I'll turn me to my faithful brute."
　　Dejectedly he turned away,
And on his horse's neck he lay
A moment :---but 'twas fatal to him,
As Slack it gave full time to view him.
And truly 'twas a gallant beast,—
Its points were to his eyes a feast :
He marked the flowing, glossy mane,
The high-arched neck, each swelling vein ;
Its small, neat head, its hazel eyes,
Which shone like stars in summer skies,
When proudly sails the Queen of Night,
Cloudless, and beautifully bright :
Yet mild withal—no vicious stare,
Nor savage glances met him there ;
But in its muscles, bone and breed,
He saw the value of the steed,
And cried, " I cant help thinkin what
A nation right slick nag you've got !

Come, let's be friends—yon shan't go yet,
And say I wouldn't stand a wet.
I aint so bad as you mout think,
But we mun live,—so let us drink!''
   He poured him out a horn brimfull
Of rum,---a spark to cheer the dull,
Cold, stolid senses of his guest,
By which he hope to warm his breast,---
Like iron heated at the fire,
To turn and mould at his desire.
   Miamo's trembling fingers clutched
The cup he never should have touched,
Unless to dash it in the face
Of him who caused his fell disgrace ;
But he had lost that self-respect
Which saves a man from cold neglect ;
Which keeps him level with his clan,
And makes him *feel* himself a *man.*
But he, poor savage, fed a fire
That grew and swelled upon desire ;
And soon did he his senses smother,
For one cup followed quick the other,
Until he had (a knave to suit,)
Sunk from a wretch into a brute.
   " Brother !'' he cried, " 'tis good ! 'tis good !
It warms my heart, and fires my blood ;
It gives me back my eagle eye,
And tells me I shall nobly die ;
Shall fight again my way to fame,
Again possess a warlike name ;
And our young men shall still admire
My speaking at the council-fire :
Our squaws shall train their young, like reeds,
To imitate Miamo's deeds ;

And Morah,---spirit of my soul !
My light ! my life ! my love ! my whole !
Oh thou no more shalt shame to own
Me as the Brave thy charms had won ;---
Shall from thy bosom banish grief,
And claim Miamo as thy chief.
Oh when I from the fight return,
And thy fond heart with joy doth burn
To hear admiring thousands raise
The song of triumph in my praise.
Wilt thou not then forget the cloud
Which for a time my fame did shroud ?
Oh yes ! thou from thy mind wilt cast,
For present joys, the gloom that's past.
Or should I on the war-path die,
Will not a tear bedim thine eye ?—
A tear thou shalt not shame to shed,
An honest tribute to the dead :
To him whose memory e'er shall have
Within thy heart a living grave "
   His eye flashed with unwonted fire,
As though he saw his soul's desire,—
His long-lost fame within his grasp ;
And forth he stretched his hand, to clasp
His honour from the empty air ;
But ah ! he clutched no honour there ;
For there, alas ! his tempter stood,
To bar him on his way to good ;
To turn him on his dark path back,
That he might follow on his track ;
To, like a serpent, surely glide,
And dart when need be to his side.
   So 'twas with Slack :—he knew his cue,
And " Bosh!" he cried, " what's here to do ?

Art gwain to tear creation up ?
Come, better have another cup,
Than be a standin, starin there,
A buildin castles in the air.
A nation lot yer gwain about,
And some fine things, there aint no doubt ;
But did ye never hear that fools
And men of sense must work with *tools ?*"
   " Thou'lt give me mine !" the Indian cried ;
   " Not I !" Elnathan Slack replied ;
" But hark ye, Redskin, this I'll do ;
I'll dicker with thee fair and true :
You see that Nag there ?—wall, look here !
I'm gwain to do the thing that's clear
And open by ye :—I'll give back
Yer plunder,* or my name aint Slack !
Aye all !—yer traps, yer bow, yer rifle,
And all for jist one downright trifle :—
That horse,—that's all !—you cant do less,—
A right good bargin, too. I guess ;
Besides yer redskin stuffed with rum
A everlastin' time to come."
   " Not so ! not so !" Miamo cried ;—
" 'Tis Morah's,—given her when a bride
By Carrib, as a dower,---Oh !
That day !---and am I sunk so low ?
That day !---it must, it shall return !
That day !---how bitterly I scorn
Myself, that could that happy day
From my fond memory chase away !
That could forget, brave Carrib's child,
Proud Morah, once on me had smiled ;

_____

Property.

Had deigned to give her virgin word,---
Had deigned to take me for her lord:
It *must* return ;---my arms !" he cried ;---
" The nag ! the horse !" his host replied.
" What's hern is yourn, dont you see ?
Therefore to sell the brute yer free :
That's jist the way where I comes from,---
A nation good way too, I vum !
You redskins make, in all besides,
To overtake us rapid strides :
But talkin's dry work, that's a fac,
So let us t'other jug attack.
Here, drink ;---we're gittin' 'tarnal low ;
And then you'll jist five dollars owe ;
And as I'm poor, and cannot trust,
You'll jist tip up the ready dust :---
Upright ! downstraight ! drag out's the way !
I'm slick for *dicker* or for pay."
" Pay !" cried the savage, with a stare---
" I told thee when I now came here,
That I no gold nor silver had ;
I came unto thee low and sad,
And drink you *gave* me,---so I thought,---
Is friendship's offering to be bought ?"
   " Oh darn that friendship !" cried out Slack:
" 'Twont put a shirt upon one's back ;---
Wont pay the ready when 'tis due,
And aint worth more than ' how d'ye do ?'
' I hopes yer well,' and all that there ;
Which aint the way to make the mare
To go, nor git the pot to bile.
I said I'd dicker, jist awhile ;
I say so still, and I will stick
To what I say through thin and thick.

D

You've heard my say.---now what say you?
Jist tell us what you mean to do."
   Poor, poor Miamo! Nature's child !
How truly is thy race called *wild !*
Or who that knew the arts that man
To catch his fellows ofttimes plan,
Could fall, as thou and thine have fell,
And scarcely left one tribe to tell
The fate of hundreds gone before?
Yea, nations, who erst proudly bore
Themselves, whilst masters of their own,
Are now extinct—for ever gone !
Plundered ! cheated ! left to die,
The victims of cupidity.
And so art thou!---torn from thy grade,
Thy bright resolves in vain were made ;
Thou shouldst have made them long ago,
When on a level with thy foe :—
Shouldst then have met him with a frown,
And kept the wily tempter down :
But now thy struggle comes too late,
Nor canst thou battle with thy fate ;
For lo! the Yankee drops the mask,
And boldly ends his irksome task :—
Doth like a skilful angler ply
Awhile with guile the gaudy fly,
Then throws aside the honest skin,
And shows the greedy wolf within.
   And poor Miamo, ere an hour,
Was wholly in Elnathan's power ;—
Coaxing, threatening, and drinking,
Soon changed his better way of thinking;
His fallen state he heeded not,
And Morah's love was all forgot ;

Her gentle steed, too, soon was lost,---
Purloined, not purchased, by his host ;
His own bright fame was offered up,
And bartered for a poisoned cup.
   Then mid-day came,---gay, soothing, bright!
All nature smiling in her might!
Her mountains, rising proudly high,
Shewed nobly 'gainst the deep-blue sky ;
Her sea-like lakes, unruffled, calm,
Bore on their crystal bosoms, balm
Shed from a thousand varied flowers,
Fair offering for the cloud-drawn showers
They had received by Zephyr borne,
Ere Phœbus rose on that fair morn.
And then her prairies, boundless plains !
Her noble rivers,---Nature's veins !
Her forest oak, her stately pines,
Each with its veil of tangled vines,
Which, net-work like, in festoons hung
On every branch, and lightly swung
When wafted by the summer breeze,
Which, sighing, glided through the trees.
   Oh! 'twas a fair scene,---passing fair!
Dame Nature had been busy there,
And lavish too,---no niggard hand
Had she held o'er that favoured land.
   But all, alas! to him was nought ;
'Twas not in Nature that he sought
To cheer his soul, or feast his mind,
As home he staggered, stupid, blind!
Bereft of all, save (fatal gift!)
His hunting-knife was all he'd left.
He thrust this 'neath his wampum belt,
Which ever and anon he felt.

As intervals of sense returned,
Or when his brain with madness burned !
Oh ! then he felt the pangs of hell,
And woke the echoes with his yell ;
Or onward plunged with savage stare,
Or right or wrong, he recked not where.

END OF CANTO THE FIRST.

CANTO II.

—◆—

" Oh grief beyond all griefs, when fate
" First leaves the young heart lone and desolate
" In this wide world, without that only tie
" For which it loved to live, or feared to die."

MOORE.

POOR Morah! who that saw thee now,
The marks of grief upon thy brow,---
Thy glossy tresses, jetty black,
In elf-locks drooping down thy back ;---
Thy once-bright eye, which star-like then
Shone as 'twill never shine again ;---
Oh! who could recognise thee now
As her, who erst with regal brow,
And queenly step, moved proudly on,
Yet blessing those thou smil'dst upon ?
Yet now no tears bedewed her eye,
Nay seldom was she heard to sigh ;
Her heart had felt too many scars,
Hers was a woe " too deep for tears."
Like to some reckless gamester, she
Had staked her all upon a die,
The cast of which was to decide
Her fate, but oh! it was denied
That she should win :—ah no! she lost,
And like some fated vessel, tossed
From crest to trough of ruthless sea,
She yielded to her destiny.

And there she sat, low, lonesome, dull,
Her cup of sadness over full ;
But like some fallen Queen she sate—
A Queen hurled from her high estate.

And now a sound salutes her ear
Of staggering footsteps drawing near ;
She knew them well, and whom they bore
So heavily to her wigwam door,
Which by a kick wide open flew,
And shewed Miamo to her view.
She shuddering rose,—he stumbled forth,
And threw himself upon the earth.

Sullen and brute-like, there he lay,
And might have slept till close of day :
But there are nerves in woman's heart,
Which for a time may bear the smart
Of wrongs, and still may beat, expand ;
But touch them with too rough a hand,
They jar, or break ;---so Morah's did ;
For 'neath her patience there was hid
An under-current, spreading wide,---
A whelming, heaving, groaning tide,
On which *conviction* now was thrown,
That broke all tender barriers down ;
Crushed every hope she might have nursed,
And told her fate had done its worst.

With stately step and flashing eye
She moved to where her husband lay,
And with no gentle hand she shook
Him, 'till the doubly-savage woke.
" How now ! how now !" he growling said,
Fierce raising up his throbbing head ;
" How now ! how now !" again he cried :—
" At dawn, Miamo," she replied —

" This dawn, ere scarce had broke the day,
Our couch you left, and *rode* away !
And now, at noon, I see you come,
With step unsteady, *walking* home !
My horse ?"—"Gone! gone !" the Indian said :—
" Then curses light upon thy head !"
Burst from her heart and from her tongue,
As from her brow her hair she flung,
And stood before the savage elf
The picture of her former self.
" Could nothing stop thy headlong course,
But thou must drink away my horse ?
My last,---my own,---my father's gift !
Look round and see what more is left,
Save thou, a dog !" She said no more,
For he had sprung up on the floor,
And by a sure-directed blow,
Full in her face, he struck her low !
His efforts loosed his hunting-knife,
Which fell near to his prostrate wife,
Who clutched it, and with Indian ire
Leapt to her feet :—her eyes flashed fire,
And mad with rage, and blind with blood,
She sprang to where Miamo stood,
And with wild random aim did dart
The fatal knife deep in his heart !
    He uttered forth a guttural sound,
Then sank a corse upon the ground.
She stood an instant, fixed, aghast,
And then—(the heat of passion past,)
She rushed and knelt beside her chief.
Unwilling to admit belief
That he was dead. She felt his brow,
But all was cold and clammy now ;---

She pressed her hand upon his breast—
'Twas warm ;—Oh then she closer pressed,
And hope glowed in her wretched heart,
As quick she tore his robes apart,
And saw---what now she understood---
That she had felt his heart's *warm blood !*
She shrieked, until the hills around
Caught and returned the piercing sound.

*   *   *   *   *   *   *   *   ‹

The council-fire that eve burnt bright,
And shed a ruddy glow of light
On faces counter-lit by fear,
That were convened together there ;
But 'twas not selfish fear did mark
Those anxious faces ;---no, each dark
And swarthy form that there had met,
Did know no self-fear ; yet they sat
Like men who tremblingly await
The word that may decide their fate.
'Twas not of war they'd met to talk,
Nor how by stratagem to baulk
A wily foe ; their hatchet long
Had buried been ;---their wild war-song
Had ceased to swell upon the air,
Yet still and anxious sat they there.
Conspicuous, too, among the rest,
Old Carrib sat ;---his manly breast
Seemed by contending feelings rent,
As each eye there was on him bent,
Beaming with expectation high ;
Yet nought was heard,—not e'en a sigh

Escaped that old man's labouring heart
As there he sat, to play the part
The Roman Brutus once had played
When he the sword of justice swayed.

An Indian Brutus,—savage,—wild,
Now sat in judgment on *his* child.

At length he spoke. " Who else," he said,
" Save me, hath on the war-path led
My Braves, these by-past forty years ?
As witness these my gaping scars !
The thieving Sioux, treacherous band,
Ne'er saw me fly, but always stand,
And front them, like a wolf at bay,
Where hottest raged the bloody fray !
I did my duty only *then*,—
I'll do my duty *now* again.

You've seen me on the hunting ground
Face danger where 'twas to be found ;---
I fled not from the buffalo's rush,
Nor shunned the fatal jungle bush ;
Where lurked the panther or the bear,
I always *led* my young men there :—
I did my duty only then !
I'll do my duty now again.

Warriors and Braves ! our laws were made
By those who long the debt have paid
Of Nature,—and have left to me,—
Their delegate,—those laws to see
Dispensed with steady, even hand,
To high or low, throughout our band :—
I *will* do so ;—our wise men said,
Let those who wilful blood shall shed
Be executed by the hand
Of him who next of kin shall stand

E

Unto the murdered man." He paused ;---
A tear stood in his eye, and caused
A dimness in his sight ; his breast
Convulsive heaved, and his broad chest
Throbbed for an instant,—then he said,
" Fetch Uncas, brother of the dead :
Go, fetch him from our hunting ground,
And tell the Brave, with gentle sound,
His kin is dead,---slain by his wife,
Who now awaits his legal knife :"
Then added, with a deep-drawn sigh,
" Maniton wills it,---she must die !"
And oh ! no friendly voice was heard
In opposition to the word,—
The fatal word that there had passed,
Dooming that day as Morah's last ;
But solemnly the Council rose,---
Each countenance in grave repose
Was wrapped, as though no dire affair
Had called them each together there !
Homeward they went, sunk deep in thought,
Which no compunction with it brought ;
Theirs were hearts in sternness steeped,---
Theirs were eyes that never wept.

But one dark form still lingered there,
That seemed to woo the cooling air,
As o'er his fevered brow it swept,
Laden with dew, as though it wept
The fate of her,—that old man's child,
Condemned, and offered up by wild
And savage laws.   His stern, dark brow,
Was all relaxed and saddened now ;
And though no tears escaped his eyes,
Yet long and frequent were the sighs

And groans that issued from his heart,
As there he stood aloof, apart
From all, till one and all were gone,
And left that old man there alone.
　And there he stood, his head declined
Unto his breast,—that noble mind
Almost a wreck ; but suddenly
Some dread resolve lit up his eye,
And strung his nerves :—he ground his teeth,
And drew, with hissing noise, his breath,
And wildly clutched at vacant air,
As though some deadly foe was there.
　Oh ! 'twas a dreadful sight to see
That frenzied old man make his way,
Rushing along the village road
To where his lonely wigwam stood :
He entered, seized his hatchet,—then
He quickly issued forth again.
　All there was hushed,—no sound was heard,
Except the wind, which slightly stirred
The summit of the leafy dome
That waved above his forest home.
He closed the door, and on he went,
Upon his deadly errand bent ;
Away he strode the village through,
Which soon had faded from his view.

*　*　*　*　*　*　*　*　*

　'Tis strange how eager some folks are
To tell ill news,—nor do they care
How fast or far they have to go,
To add unto another's woe !

'Twould seem that something very wrong
About their tell-tale natures hung;
For e'en in polished nations, too,
We find the maxim is too true!
Then who shall wonder at the speed
The Indian messenger had made,
In bounding over hill and plain
Young Unca's hunting-camp to gain?
'Twas midnight ere he found the chief,
And told his dreadful tale:—in brief,
No time was lost by Uncas there,
But like a lion from his lair
Aroused, he armed and darted forth,
With strides that seemed to spurn the earth.
　　On through the woods young Uncas ran,
With speed that only savage can;
His tangled way he homeward hied,
The stars above his only guide;
He heeded not the fearful howl
Of wolves, which in their nightly prowl
Were swiftly trotting on his trail,
With pattering feet, like falling hail!
He cared not; on like them he strode,
Like them was on the scent of blood.
He left the woods and plains behind,
Outstripped the wolves as would the wind;
Plunged from the river's rocky bank
So prone, that for a while he sank
Beneath the turbid water's breast,
That o'er him rushed with foaming crest,
Then glided past him, till at length
He rose, as with a giant's strength,
And battling with the mimic tide,
He quickly gained the other side.

There,—startled by his presence, rush
The night-birds from the neighbouring bush ;
The eagle from his eyric soared,
The cat-a-mount in discord roared ;
And rose from out the sedgy rill
The plaintive cry of " whip-poor-will."
But Uncas needed not the whole,—
Revenge and justice filled his soul !
The drenching waters from the brook
He from his garments quickly shook,
And sped him on his darksome way ;
But in his path the panther lay
Couched,—his eye-balls flashing fire,
Lashing his sides with hungry ire !—
With short, sharp growl, and head bent low,
He couched to spring upon his foe !
But Uncas, quick as lightning, drew,
His tomahawk with grasp e'er true,
Then raised it with unerring poise,
And hurled it 'twixt the flaming eyes ;
Then, with one bound, the blade regained,
And plucked it from the beast he'd brained.
Then on again,—away he hied !
He there had snuffed the crimson tied—
Hot blood had smelt, and longed for more,
Like some wild beast of Afric's shore.

END OF CANTO II.

CANTO III.

" It seemed that I stood on the verge of the tomb,
    " While the flapping of ravens I heard ;
" I felt the sweet calm between gladness and gloom,
    " And patiently waited the word."

                                        BOWRING.

Lo ! how the mountain mist now flies,
As morning opes her smiling eyes !
It rolls across the prairie plain,
Like waves along the boundless main,
Chasing with almost shadowy form
Away what seems a spectre storm !
But now its course is nearly run,—
'Tis vanquished by yon glorious sun,
Which bright as burnished gold doth shine,
Above yon groves of stately pine :
Each bird its morning matin sings,
And shakes the night-dew off its wings.
    Poor Morah ! all could not impart
One ray of joy to her lorn heart !
All there was hapless, hopeless gloom,
Like nothing save a silent tomb,
Where withers now all that which late
Did flourish in a beauteous state.
One wish alone sprang like a flower
Upon a lone and ruined tower,
Within her heart ;---it was to see
Her father, and to clasp his knee
Once more before the fatal knife
Should ease her of a weary life.

" He will not come !" the mourner said,---
" *That* hope, like others too, has fled!
Well, 'tis the last ;---I soon shall roam
Where disappointment cannot come !
No !---blighted hopes will not be found
Upon the Happy Hunting-ground ;
I soon shall lose my load of woe,
And to the Land of Spirits go !"
  A smile of resignation o'er
Her fine face spread ;---her features bore
A sunlight of approaching bliss,
A gleam of coming happiness.
  " *He* will be there, too ;---he'll be there,
But not as he, alas ! was here ;
No pale-faced villain there can come,
To wean him from his happy home !
I *shall* know joy ;—Manitou's good,
And will wash off these spots of blood !
Yes !---man may crush my outward part,
But he will judge me by the heart."
  A yell now broke upon her ear
Of wailing voices drawing near :---
They nearer drew,---she knew them well,
And recognised her own death-knell
In every note :---the door flew wide,
And "Father ! guide me !" Morah cried,
As, wildly bounding to her feet,
She forward flew, in hope to meet
Her father, but he came not there ;
She only met the sullen stare
Of savage guards, who there had come
To lead her to her early doom.
  " He will not come ! I've thrown disgrace,"
She cried, " for ever on his race,

And am become a blighted spot,
That must be wiped out and forgot!"
    She cast a suppliant gaze towards
Where silent stood the swarthy guards,
And "Braves!" she cried, " my last desire
Is, ere I die, to see my sire!
Go tell him, and my thanks receive,---
Alas! I've nothing else to give!"
"Our chief is nowhere to be found
Throughout the woods and plains around!
He has been sought for, far and near,
But he is gone, we know not where."
    " Not found!" she moaned,---" my father gone!
Then truly am I left alone!
Well,---give me up to Uncas now ;---
I'll bear without a sigh the blow
That sends me from this vale of grief,
To join my soul's once noble chief."

    They led her passively along,
Chaunting low her own Death-song.

DEATH-SONG OF THE INDIAN WIFE.

Spread now our mat, love,
    To receive me,
Where cruel fate, love,
    Will not grieve me.

I want to come love,
    And be near thee ;—
In our new home, love,
    I will cheer thee.

No pale-face there, love,
    Can seduce thee,
In his base snare, love,
    To abuse thee.

Again we'll join. love,
And for ever ;
And feel of pain, love,
Never ! never !

No more we'll part, love,
Joy partaking,
And each heart, love.
Know no aching.

When they had reached the fatal ground,
She ceased, and cast her eyes around
Upon the many faces there,
But him she sought for was not near :
But scarcely had she gazing stood
A moment, ere from out the wood
A wild yell rose upon the air,
That told of some one drawing near.
Hope once more beamed in Morah's eye,---
" I *shall* yet see him ere I die !"
She cried ;---" Manitou ! Oh for this
Thou know'st I am all thankulness !
My father ! come !" she cried aloud,
Bounding towards the yielding crowd,
Which quick fell back to form a road
For him that came, who breathless strode
Within the circle, and did grasp
Poor Morah with *no parent's* clasp.
'Twas Uncas, and a low faint cry
Escaped her as she caught his eye !
He tried to speak, but ah ! his tongue
Unnerved and motionless was hung,
Within his hot lips, parched and dried ;---
" Oh ! give me drink '" at length he cried.

They brought him full a polished shell
Of water from the bubbling well,
And deep he drank, the rest did throw
Upon his burning, fevered brow,
And " good!" he cried ; "A short relief
To soothe the bitterness of grief.
O Miamo! long-lost brother!
Hadst thou never tasted other
Beverage, save only this,
Thou hadst not tasted wretchedness ;
And thy abused, long-loving wife,
Would not have robbed thee of thy life!"
He knelt, and raised the prostrate form
Of Morah, and across his arm
She lay like one bereft of life ;
He then drew forth his hunting-knife
From out his wampum-belt, and said,
As mournfully he shook his head,
" Nor I,---oh what a task is mine !
Should not thus shed this blood of thine ! "
He with the glittering weapon, drew
A cross of blood upon her brow !
She shuddered as the pain awoke
Suspended consciousness, and spoke :
" Oh, will he come ?" she faintly said,---
" With his last blessing on my head,
I could endure with life to part ! "---
The knife that moment pierced her heart !
She shrieked ! then " Father !" gently cried,
When Carrib, bounding forth, replied,
" I come, my child ! "---fell from *the Horse,*
And threw himself upon her corse !
    It was *the Horse,*---poor *Morah's Horse,*
That stood there panting o'er her corse.

The Indians flew to aid their Chief,---
Alas! they found him past relief!
They shook him, lifted up his head,
But all was useless,---he was dead !
His dress with clotted blood besmeared,
A deep gash on his brow appeared ;
His right hand still his weapon clasped,
And in his left a *scalp* he grasped ;---
A *white man's* scalp was reeking there,
And on it *bushy sandy* hair.

It told his tale,---it told the scene,
And who the actors there had been !---
It told of watching all that night ;---
It told, too, of no bloodless fight :---
It told who fell, and who had come
To bring that reeking trophy home :---
And if, perchance, the rest should fail,
'Twill tell the *moral* of my tale.

THE END OF "MORAH."

—◆—

NUPTIAL ODE

On the Marriage of His Royal Highness the PRINCE OF WALES *to*
ALEXANDRA, PRINCESS OF DENMARK : *March* 10, 1863.

OH! for a lute-like strain
  Soft as the coo of the wooing dove,
To welcome o'er the main
  The Daughter of Britannia's love,
Our loved and lovely Dane!
Ring out! ring out the voice of gladness,
And be oh! hushed the sigh of sadness;
Lift at length the drooping head,
And mourn no more the happy dead!
The blissful living claims our voice
To shout around rejoice! rejoice!
Time is not ours to waste in grief,
  For, wait to-morrow,
And on his wings he wafts relief
  For many a sorrow!
Then let us hail him when we may,
Clothed in garb of bright array,
As on this bright nuptial day.

Lo! now he comes by Love attended,
Hymen smiling in his train,
Bright as if from heaven descended,
And by hosts of angels tended,
Guarding each his torch and chain.
And Nature wakes from Winter's cold embrace
Each smiling child of ever-welcome Spring ;
The daffodil, first-born of Flora's race,
Doth round about its garish beauties fling !
And lo! is here the modest violet,
Sweet type of England's early-wedded bride ;
And, by its side,
The primrose. with Aurora's gems bewet,
Smiles in its pride—
Smiles in its pride to deem it may
Join to greet our nuptial day.

Hark! hark! what joyful sounds are here,
Swelling over hills and dales,
With sweet notes, now low, now clear,
Faintly distant.—gayly near !—
'Tis the harp of happy Wales!
Yes, Cambria's bards their Prince's nuptial day
Hail each with heart and harp in blissful lay—
In blissful lay,
Which seems to say,
Hail to our Prince's nuptial day !

And Erin, sweet Erin, green isle of the ocean,
Joins with her soul and her harp in the throng ;
Lealy and loudly, with joyful emotion,
Ever the first in the heart-stirring song !

Up from each valley, and down from each mountain,
Round each blue lake, from the lip of each fountain,
Swells the gay chorus, so widely recounting
  The joy that is felt on this bright nuptial day.

  And auld acquaintance, Scotia's Muse,
    Now smiles and weeps in turns,
  To think that she ha' no' the noo
    Her darlin' Rabbie Burns!
  For he would be the chiel to chaunt
    A cheerfu' winsome lay,
  And gie a sang wad warm each heart
    On this our nuptial day'
  But cheerly yet, oh! cheerly yet,
    For mony do we fin'
  To tune the pipes with hearty will.
    As auld lang syne.

  Hark, the merry bells are ringing,
    And the birds on every tree,
  From matin until vesper singing,
    Adding to the nation's glee!
    Swelling wide our wedding glee!
  All, all rejoice them as they may,
  On this our Prince's nuptial day.

A CHAPTER ON COATS.

Some folks still move upon the plan
That 'tis " the tailor makes the man ;"
That nothing can be worth two groats
Produced by those in threadbare coats.
A being, by such, a man is not
Considered, if he has not got
Upon him, or of black or blue,
Fine cloth an extra yard or two.
It seems they have been reading wrong
The words of Scotia's Son of Song,
By whom 'twas thought, we had been told,
That *manhood* was the sterling gold,—
That " rank " and riches were just but
The " stamp " upon the metal put!
But worth is now but seldom thought
To dwell within a threadbare coat.

Just take a male, or young or old,
It matters not, so he has gold ;
Complexion may be dark or fair,
Or as a badger grey his hair ;
Yet if he has but got the " brass "
In purse *and face*, he'll surely pass ;—
Will pass for what men call a " buck,"
Or what the ladies term a " duck !"
But oft their " duck," as all have heard,
Has proved a *somewhat larger* bird,
When ladies wed, have turned their " ducks,"
By some strange means, back into *bucks*.

But puns are things I dont play on,
So with the subject will have done;
I only up the subject brought
To prove that manhood's *not* the coat.

Well; money, (people tell us so)
Will always "make the mare to go!"
But still, 'twill never make, of course,
Howe'er we try, a silken purse
From out a goodly porker's ear,—
That fact, I ween, is pretty clear.
Suppose we for example take
One eminent in church or state,
But who, from out of all his wealth,
Did never yet "do good by stealth,"
Or publicly affix his name,
Lest he should " blush to find it fame,"
Can station, wealth, or even both,
Tho' backed by coat of finest cloth,
Make such an one, on any plan,
A Christian?—nay, or even *man?*
No, never! Learning, riches, dress,—
All these, than man would make him *less!*
It is for *deeds*, not coats and words,
That man to man *manhood* awards!
Let him be rich, or *sans* a groat,
The " man's the man," and not the coat.

MAY-DAY.

Oh! 'tis May-day,
Once a gay day,
Warming the hearts of old and young!
Bells were ringing,
Birds were singing
" Right merrilie " their gush of song!
Eyes were glancing,
Feet were dancing,
E'en everywhere the meads among.

And, here, upon the village green,
Spruce lads and lasses might be seen,
All tripping round the Maypole gay,
And chasing Time and care away—
Care that crushes oft amain,
And Time that never comes again.
The bull that to the ring was tied,
Now lashed with pain his panting side;
Whilst noble dogs he, here and there,
Gored to the earth, or tossed in air;
The while the peasant and the squire
Would bull now cheer, then dogs admire.
Oh! for a burning Muse to praise,
In song of fire, the "good old days."
Bold chanticleer his meed did yield
Of sport upon the battle field;
With close-clipped wings, and spurs of steel
Bound firmly round his ready heel;
Thus armed, he meets his willing foe,
And hurls him back his blow for blow;

And soon were seen the gory plume,
The 'sanguined spur and ragged comb!
Rapid and fell the passes are,
As shouts and oaths rise on the air.
" Curse you! touch not again my bird!"
Above the din is hoarsely heard.
" I backed the red!" another cries;
" You lie! you lie!" his friend replies;
" You backed the blue,—the bird now down,
So hand me quickly up my crown!"
Blows now from brawny arms are given,
And, for a moment, back is driven
A portion of the savage crew,
(The birds, meanwhile, both lost to view);
But, reinforced, back to the fray
Crowds rush, and hit whom hit they may!
The heavy hedge-stakes, crushing down,
Lay bare full many a bleeding crown,
Whilst stones fly round as thick as hail,
As *red* or *blue* may each assail.
And where the birds? In mercy trod
To shapeless masses in the mud!
Oh! for a burning Muse, to praise,
In song of fire the "good old days."

Ah me! what have we now to show,
In early May, to friend or foe?
The foe, (if foe there dare to be),
No doubt would still prefer to see
Us still engaged in rivalry!
And so we are, but not, as once,
The brute to brute, and dunce to dunce;
But bounding youth contend for fame
In our most noble cricket game

And spreading now our commons o'er,
Is seen a gallant rifle corps,
Each emulous which best shall stand
"To guard from foes our native land;"
And friends—well-wishers of their kind—
What change more grateful can such find,
Than almost everywhere is found
Where teems a well-tilled plot of ground?
And even rivalry is there,
For each one strives his best to rear
The choicest flower, or earliest fruit,
The fullest plant, or soundest root;
And maid and matron, child and wife,
All gaily join the friendly strife.
Oh! for a living Muse, to praise,
In lasting verse, our *modern Mays.*

NOTE.—The cock-fight scene, which I have but faintly described
above, I was a witness of in my boyhood's days, and which " came
off" within fifty miles of Lugwardine.—AUTHOR.

THE WORLD'S FAIR—AN ODE.

FAME, seated on her modern throne,
    Supported by Britannia's hand,
Blasts from her clarion loud hath blown,
    Wide-sounding over sea and land!

A voice hath gone forth from the south to the north,
    And a voice from the east to the west;
It speaketh to all to whom speaking is worth,
    To the sons of the earth e'en the best:—

To those to whose talent and labour are owing
  The fruits of the soil and the wealth of the deep;
Even to those who too-often employed are in sowing
  The seeds which in yielding-time others doth reap.

Such hear the sound, and to our shores
  Bring from afar their treasured stores ;
The stores by gold alone ne'er bought,
The mind-drawn, priceless " gems of thought ;"
E'en such as polished minds produce
At once for ornament and use.

Fame too long her trump hath sounded,
  Soaring 'bove the crimson car,
As on o'er slaughtered heaps it bounded,
As on it drove o'er dead and wounded,
  Lying low on fields of war !

Long, too long, has peaceful Science
  Dreamt of honours on her brow ;
Placed on *use* her sole reliance,
To bid unto the sword defiance,
  As she leant on loom or plough ;
    But loom and plough
    Have proved till now,
    Like peaceful word
    Has to the sword,
A subject-matter, wherein Right
Has silenced been by tyrant Might ;
  But rightful Might—Utility—
    Stands forth at length,
    To show her strength,
  And prove the mind's nobility.

Oh, what can come from points or south or north,
Or east or west, that England brings not forth ?

We may not show the baubles of the East,
Nor yet display the virgin gold of West ;
But, let Wisdom hold the scales with even poise,
    Reject the chaff, and weigh the sterling corn :
Proclaim aloud her clear, impartial choice,
    And mark where Fame will point her golden horn.

O Britain ! bright garden for useful uprearing,
    For staple commodities second to none ;
With climate of south and of north, midway sharing
    In equal proportions the smiles of the sun.

Embedded beneath thy broad bosom abideth
    Rich ores, and which Science upturneth with ease ;
Whilst Commerce, with wind-like rapidity glideth
    O'er iron-ribbed earth and obedient seas.

Thy sons—let them plough, pen, or pencil be wielding,
    Will vie with the best, come they near or from far ;
In Science and Art the palm will not be yielding,—
    Will conquer in peace as they've vanquished in war.

Yet hush ! a dirge-like wail, wierd in its tone,—
Like moan of spirits wandering wide and lone,
Seeking their lost as those who seek in vain,—
Floats through the aisles, a sad, yet holy strain.
What form is she who moves with downcast eye,
And breasts up-heaving with the burstnig sigh ?
Bare are her arms, and her dishevelled hair
Floats freely wild upon the wanton air !
Sons press around her 'neath that glittering dome,
Who hither north, south, east, and west have come
            To do her homage there !
Yet Art ! O Art ! well mayst thou sigh,
And wander on with downcast, weeping eye,
For lost ! for ever lost, thy gifted son !

And see, where weeping near,
Sad Science with slow step doth move,
  With, following in her train,
The Genius of Domestic Love,
  Who never shall again,
With kindling eye, e'er gaze upon
Our Albert gone! for ever gone!

SOLITUDE.

The Bard's Apology for Murmuring.

WHO loves thee with a heart attuned to love,
    Sad Solitude?
Lay bare to human view thy choicest charms,
Or deck thee in thy gaudiest bravery,
    Still thou art rude!
For, even then, thou wilt but plainly prove
Less easier borne than even hapless love,
    Or midnight cry of war's alarms,
    Or chained and fettered slavery!
The mind—the strongest mind—will pale to face
The long, long vista of unbounded space;
Just as the sinking soul will shrink to fly
From narrow Time to wide Eternity.
Though round the ruined heart no ivy clings,
Nor flowers blossom in revolving springs,
Whose conscience bears no cicatrice of crime,
Yet pales at past and dreads the future time!
Yet Hope, sweet Hope, the wretch's morning dream,
Sheds o'er such hearts an undefined gleam,
Points to dim distance, where, in rainbow hues,
Shine faintly fair some oft-dissolving views;
Bright, now, as morn, (Hope's parent, ever dear);
Now, gay as noon, when skies are bluely clear;

Then faint, alas ! and distant far away,
Like the dull tints of darkening day's decay.
   And such a hope will sometimes o'er me come—
A hope that 1 might once more find a home,
A "rod of ground,"—a roof where I might bring
Again my callow brood beneath my wing ;
And I will teach them twitter forth a prayer
For those whose kindness placed them safely there.
   The first-made man found not e'en Paradise
To be that earthly heaven—a home !—his voice
Fell not where human voice should ever fall
On human ear !—the birds, beasts, fishes, all
Were wed unto their kind ; but man, lorn man,
Alone excluded seemed from Nature's plan,
Till woman rose,—his God-made mate,—to shed
Her smile reviving on his drooping head !   [grove
Earth then seemed Heaven ! yes, e'en the deepest
Shone radiant with the sun of woman's love ;
And where before were darkness, doubt and gloom,
Bliss built her bower, and leal love called it home.
   And such mine Eden was, but withered now
My humble roof-tree, root, and branch and bough ;
And scattered those—too soon, alas ! too soon—
Whose presence made each month a month of June,
And left me here to shiver life away
In one long dull and dark December day.
Then you who sympathise will wonder not
That I should *sometimes* mourn my fallen lot ;
As not for self---oh ! not for me alone
Do I this saddening desolation moan ;
But eke for those who should on me depend,
As father, guide,---in fine, their natural friend !
And trust I will, when clouds shall pass away,
Smile when 1 can, be happy when I may.

PUGILISM AND POETRY.

A CHEER for the brawn,---the sinew and bone
   That bides in an Englishman's arm!
That is, if hard muscle and sinew alone
Will guard from all danger our altar and throne,
   Then give them a cheer wide and warm;
Yet 'tis not empty cheers alone we give
To those who might the hardest blows receive;
Nor yet to those whose wishes most incline
How best to smash the "human face divine!"
No! silver cups and belts of jewell'd gold
We give, with purses cramm'd with coin untold,
And compliment'ry benefits "get up,"
At which to give or "purse," or "belt," or "cup."
He is the hero, worthy such reward,
Who can break through his strong opponent's guard,
Can hit and stop, or right and left let fly
Bang on his adversary's mouth or eye;
Can draw "first blood," or with aim high or low
Can strike the first tremendous "knock-down blow!"
'Tis worth a silver cup to "Bill" or "Bob,"
If either gets his adversary's "nob"
In what is called in doubtful mockery,
That grip tremendous, direful "chancery."
See you poor wretch,---a loving sister's brother,
The darling son, too, of a doting mother;
His face scarce human, knocked so out of shape,
As to beseem a savage, conquered ape!
And yet some hours ago he proudly strode
That ring within,---the image of his God!

H

Yet now behold him tottering here and there,
Still striking, feebly wild, he knows not where,
Until at length,---his face one bleeding wound,
He prostrate sinks upon the gory ground.

*   *   *   *   *   *   *   *   *

There is a charm in change so that'it be
A change of scene from vice and villany ;
So view, my friends, what next I'll cause to pass,
Before your ken, in my poetic glass.
See yon poor room, (and many such there are),
Of comfort scant, and garnitnre most bare!
With no ' best vintage,' ' punch,' or ' bottled stout,'
Is yonder table fully furnished out ;
Nor do you hear a hearty shout to bring
That room within, a hero of the " ring !"
No !---no hero he who sitting there alone,
We cast our nearly careless gaze upon.
And yet he hero is, contending " left and right,"
With this strange world,---a most unequal fight ;
Unequal, for he has but sense refined
To pit against (too oft) a senseless mind :
And oft 'tis seen that brutal ignorance
Is far " too much " for even common sense.
But shall it still be seen that, midst the cry
For spread of " intellectuality ;"---
For " social science" and the wealth of mind,
            That wealth of mind
            Shall only find
    Itself beat back, to clear the way
    For brutal force in this world's fray ?
No ! woman---man---yea, even God forbid,   [hid,
That heaven-born gifts should 'neath dark clouds be
Whilst those of earth shall grasp on every hand,
As oft they do, the fatness of the land.

MY FATHER'S SWORD.

In days gone by, when Freedom's foes
  Marched boldly forth in proud array,
Britannia's free-born sons arose
  To beat them back their hostile way!
With them my noble father rode,
  To seek the soldier's best reward,
But by his side a boy I stood,
  While clasped he on his well-tried sword.

"Farewell! dear boy!" my father cried;
  "I go to win for thee a name,
That shall for ever be allied
  To honour pure and brightest fame!
I have not much I can bequeath
  To thee except the world's good word;
That shall be thine, boy, at my death,
  And this, my yet unsullied sword."

Such were the words,---and, oh, the last,
  I ever heard my father say!
For from my ardent gaze he passed
  To fight in lands far, far away!
And there he found an honoured grave,
  Receiving e'en the foe's good word,
And sent me by his comrades brave,
  His dying blessing and his sword.

His blessing I remember still,
  And shall until my dying day,
And on his weapon read his will,---
  A sacred charge I now obey!
For at my country's call " to arms,"
  I grasp it with a glad accord,
And when amidst wild war's alarms,
  I'll not disgrace my father's sword.

CAST AWAY.

Ah! dost thou think I have no heart, love,
  Beating in this breast of mine?
That coldly thus with me you part, love,
  Knowing me so wholly thine?
Ah! Mary! think, dear, of to-morrow,
  If thou canst forget to-day!
Dream a day-dream, love, of sorrow,
  For a leal heart thrown away---
             Cast away!
     Ever more to pant for thee,
     Never more at peace to be.

Ah! once I dreamt a blissful dream, love;
   Dreamt of happy days to come;
I saw thee, like a bright sun-beam, love,
   Shining in my manhood's home!
But sure I slept when vows of love, dear,
   Seemed a pleasing theme to thee,
When beneath sweet Belmont's grove, dear,
   Late we paced the banks of Wye---
                Banks of Wye--
      Happy there I dwelt with thee,
      In a sweet futurity.

'Twas then I thought that I could trace, love,
   As I gazed enraptured there,
On thy upturned smiling face, love,
   The end of all my youthful care!
But all my hopes are changed to sorrow
   And woe—not only for to-day,
But for many a sad to-morrow,
   Since my leal heart's thrown away—
                Cast away,
      Evermore to pant for thee,
      Never more at rest to be.

SOME OF THESE DAYS.

Oh, Mary! dear Mary, you say I seem sad,
   And wonder I laugh not and joke as of old;
That at evening I meet thee no longer the lad
   You knew me but lately so gallant and bold!
I am not the same, sweet, I will not deny,
   Tho' why I am changed, and so altered my ways,
The reason I smile not when you, dear, are by,
   Is a secret I'll tell you, love, some of these days.

You remember the dance, where I led thee, the while
  Young Will of the Mill looked so gloomily down?
I saw that you met his dark look with a smile,
  That told me how little you cared for his frown!
Oh! I felt something then, which I feel even now,
  For morn, noon, and night on my spirit it preys;
I can guess what it is, and if you will allow
  'Tis a secret I'll tell you, love, some of these days.

'Twas but lately I loved, dear, to range o'er the hills,
  Or to wander alone beneath Dinedor's cool shades,
And to sing to the music that rose from the rills,
  As they rippled, half hid, through the neighbouring
    glades!
But I now care no longer alone, love, to roam,
  'Neath the shadows of eve nor the moon's cheering
    rays;
And why I am sad in my bachelor home,
  Is a secret I'll tell you, love, some of these days.

LADIES' WILLING FINGERS—A SONG FOR CRIMEAN HEROES.

Air—"*Green grow the Rushes, O.*"

Come, comrades! pass the can about,
  And hark whilst I shall sing here, O!
And you a chorus loud must shout
  Will make the welkin ring here, O!
My theme is one that all must own
  All other themes surpasses, O!
So let us join our shouts as one,
  In cheers for British lasses, O!

CHORUS.

When messmates bled, and comrades died,
    It yet in memory lingers O!
How here at home, for us they plied
    Their little willing fingers, O!

Yes; were they cottage lasses bred,
    Or tender high-bred maidens, O!
Or mothers, matronly and staid,
    Or little romping hoydens, O!
Yet one and all, with hand and heart,
    Sat down for us to labour, O!
And each one tried to do her part
    Much quicker than her neighbour, O!

Poor Polls, who'd not much time to spare,
    And sweet Miss Janes, with leisure, O!
Wrought each for us their utmost share,
    And thought it quite a pleasure, O!
They only thought how hard our fate,
    Half naked in the passes, O!
And early toiled for us and late,
    Like gallant British lasses, O!

Oft roared the thunders o'er our head,
    The rain in torrents falling, O!
And round us rattled storms of lead,
    Our hearts almost appalling, O!
Yet on we rushed, for well we knew
    Warm hearts with us were sharing, O!
Though far, far o'er the waters blue,
    The dangers we were daring, O!

Should war's wild sounds again alarm
  The tender heart of woman, O!
We'll up again with heart and arm,
  And beat again the foeman, O!
God bless the lasses, rich and poor!
  And in their youth and old years, O!
Repay their kindness evermore
  To war-worn British soldiers, O!

    When messmates bled and comrades died,
      It yet in memory lingers, O!
    How here, at home, for us they plied
      Their little willing fingers, O!

LUGA'S PRIDE—SWEET MARY.

PASTORAL BALLAD.

HARD by where Luga gently glides,
  My Mary, to the world unknown,
In yonder cottage coyly hides
  The beauty that would grace a throne,
      So lovely is my Mary!
Nor would she lose, though low her birth,
  If fate e'en now should place her there,
One impulse of her inward worth,
  Nor of her grace one outward air,
      So void of pride is Mary.

  Though radiant as the blush of day,
    Her lowly state she ne'er forgets;
  Nor throws she e'er a thought away
    In wishes wild or vain regrets,
      So happy is my Mary.

I've heard the lark at early morn,
　At eve sweet Philomela's tongue,
But neither to my ear hath borne
　Such music as my lassie's song,
　　　　So blithesome is my Mary.

And oh! what pride, what bliss is mine,
　To know myself the favoured youth,
To whom such sweetness doth incline
　With fervent and depending truth,
　　　　So artless is my Mary!
And well do I, each coming day,
　Improve my time, to make me all
That he should be who shortly may
　Himself the happy husband call
　　　　Of Luga's pride, sweet Mary!

And then. although no bells may ring,
　Nor gala mark the joyful tide,
I proudly to my home will bring,
　With ringing heart, my blooming bride,
　　　　Of Luga's pride, my Mary!
And she, dressed in her humble best,
　Her eyes lit up with beaming love,
A charm will light within my breast
　That shall a life-long gala prove
　　　　To me and to my Mary.

SCOTCH BALLAD—
" When truth's in the heart, there's nae harm in a kiss."

O mither ! dear mither, tho' 'tis gane sae lang
    Sin' the day when my fayther cam' to thee to woo,
Thou hastna forgotten the days thou wert young,
    Nor art thou forgettin' how young people loo.
I mind weel, dear mither, the joy that has played
    Roun' your een as ye've crackt o' the days o' yer
        bliss ;
I mind how to gossips sae aft thou hast said, [kiss."
    " When truth's i' the heart there's na wrang in a

I weel ken young Colin is leal in his loe—
    Lang sine has the laddie dear silently sued ;
But na word o' his pain did he tell me till noo,
    Tho' his een hae sa lang and respectfully wooed ;
But this eve while the tears in his blue een did stan',
    He said it wad turn a' his waes into bliss,
If I'd let him, crave o' thee, dear mither, my han' ;
    When I said that he might, 'twas he gave me the
        kiss.

My heart wad bin stane-cald, an' blind bin my e'e
    No' to ken, no' be feelin' the worth o' sic truth ;
'Twad ha' gi'en to my sex and to nature the lee,
    By graftin' weak age on the strength o' my youth.
Thou art smilin', dear mither, an' muckle I'm glad
    To ken that ye tak no' his wooin' amiss ;
An' when he comes to thee, thoul't say to the lad
    " When truth's in the heart, there's na harm in
       a kiss."

BALLAD—
LIKE THE WYE MY LOVE SHALL BE.

———◆———

SEE, love, where glides our own sweet Wye,
  Ever constant, dearest Mary;
Lingering rock and boulder by,
  Wooing ever, never weary!
Clinging round, with fond embrace,
  The verdant banks that press her nearer,
And smiling there, with dimpled face,
  Where love, half met, makes love the dearer.

Nor doth sweet Vaga shun the shore
  Made dark by wood and grove, my Mary;
But gliding nearer, smiles the more,
  To make each gloomy spot less dreary!
In sun and shade by night and day,
  Ever constant, weary never;
Passing life in love away,
  Flows our gently-wooing river.

And, like the Wye, my love shall be
  True to thee, my dearest Mary;
And such the love I sue from thee,
  Ever constant, never weary!
Should woe assail, thoul't find me near,
  To soothe thee in thy hour of sadness,
To wipe away each starting tear,
  And cheer thy drooping heart to gladness.

SONG—LADIES' NOSES.

POETS laud to the skies
Ladies' beautiful eyes,
And their cheeks, they say, rival the roses;
But I think it a sin
No one should put in
A word now and then for their noses!
Yet charms they display,
Each deserving a lay,
Far more than the thoughtless supposes;
But all will, I trow,
This one fact allow,
That girls would be "frights" without noses.

With the neck of a swan,
And the foot of a fawn,
That scarce bends the flower it presses;
And likewise the brow,
Pure as lilies or snow,
Encircled by beautiful tresses!
Yet what man would care
For a garden most rare,
That wanted the chief of its posies?
And the same should we miss,
(When the lasses we kiss)   [noses.
In the "soft blush" and "sweet scent" of their

Would their richly-stored mind
In our heart of hearts find
The throne made for maidens by nature,
If the dear ones, alas!
Could not show on their face
That pretty, though under-praised feature?

No ! the heart, that best charm,
Might be lovingly warm,
Yet I vow by " the body of Moses ! "
They never could move
A return of their love,
Had they lost but an inch of their noses.

Then while some in lays
Such like beauties may praise
As the ankle, brow, waist, or the bosom,
The eye, lip, or teeth,
Or their sweet balmy breath,
Oh! let me be the poet to *nose* 'em.
Let them be pink or pale,
Or as brown as old ale,
Or as red as the reddest of roses.
Still I'll shout like a man,
And drink when I can
All hail to the girls and their noses !

WHERE DO THE FAIRIES DWELL?

" WHERE, mother, do the fairies dwell ?
I've sought them in the shady dell ;
Have roamed the forest through and through,
And walked the morn the meadows, too ;
At eve I've paced beside the rill
That winds adown the wooded hill ;
But never, mother, could I tell
The haunts wherein the fairies dwell.

" I've heard you say the rings were bright
Whereon they've danced the live-long night !

Such rings in meadows have I seen—
The grass around a brighter green;
And yet it did not seem the sod
By dancing footsteps had been trod;
Then, dearest mother, do me tell
The haunts wherein the fairies dwell.

" You oftimes say, my mother dear,
That like a fairy, I appear,
When I so lightly trip along,
And carol forth my merry song!
And that is why I want to trace
The playful fairies sporting place,
That I may try if I as well
Can dance wherein the fairies dwell."

" My child, where such as you abound,
There always will be fairies found!
For children, as they trip along,
And carol forth their gleeful song,
Give music sweeter than the strain
Born only of the poet's brain;
For only can the poet tell
The haunts wherein the fairies dwell.

SONG — MARY AND JOHN.

You know merry Mary, late Maid of the Mill,
    Who wed with the miller's man, John;
She dwells at the cot near the foot of yon hill,
    As blest as the queen on her throne!
And 'tis just a twelvemonth last Valentine's day,
    Since the twain have been wed into one,
Yet no pair more happy, as neighbours all say,
    Together than Mary and John.

All day Mary sings, " Who so happy as I ?"
   (A song labour much will relieve,)
And greets, with a heart-cheering smile in her eye,
   Her work-weary husband at eve !   [till dark,
Oh ! 'twere worth working for, e'en from daylight
   To have such a cot for my own ;
And labour I would, love, as brisk as a lark,
   Were we married like Mary and John.

Yet Mary was fearful a twelvemonth ago
   Of changing her maiden estate,
Lest less of life's weal, love, and more of its woe
   Should fall, like a blank, to her fate !
Yet a prize has it proved, as it ever will prove,
   To those who have hearts wed as one !
And so 'twould with us, dear, if me you could love,
   And marry as Mary did John.

LOVE SONG.

I NEVER wished for worldly wealth,
   Nor hoped for fleeting fame,
Till thy sweet glance o'er my sad heart
   Like softened sunbeams came :
But would the Fates propitious prove,
   And Fortune smile on me,
I then would tell how much rich love
   Beats in this breast for thee,
              Sweet maid ;
   And beats for only thee.

Thy sunny smile—thy soft, sweet smile
  Is beaming o'er me now ;
And see I can thy rich dark hair
  Embrace thy marble brow ;
And still my thirsting memory sips
  The draught of balmy breath,
That once I drank from thy sweet lips,
  And will do till my death,
           Dear maid ;
  And will do till my death.

Ah ! yes—my heart was weary, dear,
  Of beating all alone,
And longed to pour its treasures out
  Some genial heart upon ;
Then came thy smile—thy sunny smile,
  That beams upon me yet,
And sheds upon my heart a charm
  I never shall forget,
           Sweet maid ;
  I never shall forget.

Yet nothing hast thou, love, to fear ;
  Then hide not from my view ;
For I have never dreamt a thought
  That meant a wrong to you !
No ! tho' I ne'er may hope from thee
  One fond and chaste embrace,
Yet could I live my life away
  In gazing on thy face,
           Sweet maid,
  In gazing on thy face.

SONG—MAN WAS MADE TO LOVE.

"Man was made to mourn."—BURNS.

No! no! man was not made to mourn,
  Or why is earth so fair?
Why cheerly pipe the birds at morn,
  Or fragrance fill the air?
The very flowers that deck the way,
  In garden, field, and grove,
Whilst sweetly blushing, seem to say
  That man was made to love.

No! no! man was not made to mourn,
  Or why yon glorious ray
That gilds the mountain tops at morn,
  And smiling greets the day?
And when, at eve, sweet Philomel
  Awakes the nodding grove,
In each sweet song he seems to tell
  That man was made to love.

No! no! man was not made to mourn,
  Or why yon beauteous maid?
Were such create to roam forlorn
  Without our tender aid?
Ah no! their beauties e'er must tell,—
  Where'er their footsteps move,—
More plain than song of Philomel,
  That man was made to love.

K

THE QUEEN, GOD BLESS HER!

—•—

Come, fill up a bumper, and this be the toast—
    The Queen of these Realms let us give,
And no one of British extraction dare boast,
    Who long doth not hope she may live!
But ready and steady let each of us stand,
    To drive back whate'er may oppress her,
And Echo bear swiftly this toast through the land,
    "Here's a health to the Queen, God bless her."

Let opposite factions unite in one cause,
    And strive who her smiles most may win,
By firmly supporting dear Liberty's laws,
    Which unity only can gain!
And while peace and concord are easily bought,
    Oh! let not sedition distress her;
But fill up your glasses, and drink from the heart,
    "Here's a health to the Queen, God bless her."

May her reign be recorded the epoch of bliss;
    By each monarch her glories be seen,
And tell them the way to have pleasure like this,
    Is to imitate England's fair Queen!
May her diadem sit on her brow ever light;
    May the cares of this world ne'er distress her;
And when at the last she ascends from our sight,
    With a crown everlasting God bless her!

END OF THE SONGS AND BALLADS.

THE APPARITION;

A TALE OF HEREFORD; FOUNDED ON FACT.

THE following mysterious incident (for Tale it can hardly be called) was witnessed not only by the writer, but by two other young men likewise—young men we were at the time to which I allude; our respective ages being about 18, 19, and 20—myself the oldest of the three.

Were I to be asked why, if I thought the affair of so singular a nature, I had not given it to the world before?—my reply is simply this,—the occurrence was, it is true, of too striking a character not to stamp its *main features* too deeply on my mind for time ever to erase the impression thereof! but distrusting my own memory, so far as regards *minute detail*, I was anxious, ere I gave the matter publicity, to " compare notes " with one or both of my old companions alluded to above, and who, with me, witnessed the strange fact I am about to relate.

One of my companions, whose name was Thomas Price, by trade a cabinet-maker, has been, I believe, in America these last sixteen or seventeen years, consequently I have had no opportunity to consult with him on the subject—the other (better known to my local readers), was my youth's friend and companion, the late Mr. Daniel Powell : he, likewise, had not resided in Hereford for a long time until he came, alas! to end his days among us, some few years back. Du-

ring his last illness, poor fellow, I had several conver-
sations with him on the subject ; and so far from
having had occasion to doubt the strength of my own
memory, he confirmed me in every particular it had
retained. His testimony, coming, as it did, from one
who knew his own end approaching, will, I should
hope, be duly appreciated by the reader.

It was not till after I had published my fifth pam-
phlet-poem that Powell re-appeared among us. I had
lent him copies of the whole five to read, and on his
returning them to me, he was the first to speak of my
giving the present subject publicity.

" I have been thinking, old friend," he said, " that
our Above-Eign Ghost Adventure would be an excellent subject for your next poem."

I explained to him my intention with regard to the
matter, just as I have to the reader ! but I told him
that I would not be trammelled with rhyme, and that
I would rather state the affair in plain prose.

Daniel Powell was, at the date of our adventure,
apprenticed to a respectable watchmaker, then resid-
ing in Broad-street, in this city, and was, I believe,
nearly out of his time. We---(that is to say, myself,
Powell, Price, and several other companions), had met
in the High-town (as was usual in that day), to chat
away the last half of our dinner hour, when Powell
mentioned to us the fact that he was going that same
evening to the village of Byford, in order, as he said,
to transact the monthly business of a Clock-and-
watch Club established there by his Master.

" I should," he said, " like to have a couple of you
chaps along with me, just for company sake ; I can
promise you a good supper," he added, " when you
are there, and your skins full of good cider, to boot."

This was some inducement, no doubt; but the chief one arose (as the reader will imagine with youths of our age) from the prospect held out to us of having a night's "lark." I, for one, volunteered on the instant; Price, also, was equally willing; so that the "party" was made up then and there. Having decided on the time and also the place of meeting, and "two o'clock" ringing out from steeple and tower— proclaiming that dinner-hour was passed, we parted.

It was six o'clock on the same evening that we met, and set out on what promised to be a pleasant trip. It was in the middle of summer, and the evening was as beautiful as heart could wish. It might, perhaps, have proved somewhat over warm to those who might have had an equal number of miles to walk in a less given time; but with time we had nothing to do, otherwise than to while it away as best we could; and the health, youth, and spirits we then possessed, would have borne us along, unflagged, through a walk of far more than seven miles. I have no recollection of any thing transpiring during our walk to Byford, that would be of interest to the general reader; I perfectly well remember, though, that sundown found us snugly ensconced within the hostelry known as the "Byford Boat," and discussing therein the merits of a splendid dish of eggs and bacon! In so far, then, had our friend, poor Dan, fulfilled his promise of a "good supper." During the time we were going through the above-mentioned rather agreeable performance, the members of the Club had assembled, and after it had concluded, their business was duly gone into. This did not occupy much time, and being over, we resolved ourselves into a kind of rural "free-and-easy," when songs, glees, duets, etc. (we *could* sing), wiled

away a couple of hours " ryghte merrilie." Not being
used to midnight revels, it was not more than eleven
o'clock when we broke up, and with " good night,
all's well," started for home.

The moon was just rising when we commenced our
homeward walk, and we had not progressed far ere
her beautiful beams made night almost as bright as
day ! Indeed the journey home promised to be even
more pleasant than was our walk when we were " outward bound ;" inasmuch as what little air was stirring
rendered the atmosphere delightfully cool. One little
bit of mischief occurred, I well remember, when we
had arrived opposite to the fifth mile-post : one of our
party, not having a wholesome fear of the Turnpike
Trust floating before his mental vision, picked up a
large stone and hurled it at the upper part of the post
with such force as to strike the cross-board free from
its fixture, and send it spinning far into the field beyond. We were each of us vexed at this, and none
more so than the delinquent himself : indeed, he was
not only vexed, but also quite astonished at the result
of his random exploit ;—for, on being remonstrated
with, he declared that he had not the slightest idea
that he *could* have struck the mark. " There is not,"
he said, " I should think, a worse marksman than
myself breathing; and I do believe," he added, " that
I might have stood here, pelting for an hour in the
open daylight, without striking either the post or the
board ! "

The reader may be very well excused if, after con-
ning the above, he should come to the conclusion that
we were rather the worse for what cider we had im-
bibed ; nevertheless, I must declare that such was not
the case. The freak was executed merely on the im-

pulse of the moment, prompted, no doubt, by the (to us) novelty of the situation in which we were placed. However, a rather rapid walk for the next mile or so, was the consequence.

We were at that time, with others of our young companions, studying the drama of the "Brigand," and which we played at our theatre some time afterwards as an amateur performance; and for the next two miles we amused ourselves by reciting the dialogue and singing the music of that once-popular piece. This occupied our time until we had arrived within about two miles of the city.

As the reader has, no doubt, oftentimes travelled *in imagination*, he will easily understand what I mean when I beg that he will allow me to leave my companions for a time, and accompany me onwards to within the suburbs of our ancient city. This is necessary in order that he may be made acquainted with the locality in which we witnessed the strange Apparition to which I shall presently have to call his attention.

The Above-Eign, at the time I speak of, was very unlike what that pleasant suburb is in the present day. To say that a vast improvement has not been effected in that neighbourhood, would be to state the thing that is wrong;—at the least so far as *personal* comfort extends; for, where once was spread before us little better than a rude scene of hedge, dyke, and meadow land, now neatly-built cottages—each surrounded by its trimly-kept garden-plot—greet the passer's gaze. It is to be regretted, tho', that a little more *uniformity of design* had not been agreed upon by the various owners of these pretty-looking tenements, ere they had commenced building, so that the

scene might have been rendered more picturesque as
a whole! I never look upon them without fancying
that they resemble a group of pretty girls turning the
" cold shoulder" to, and otherwise *pouting* at each
other.

It will be remembered by many of my local readers
that, at the time to which I refer, in front of the spot
where these freehold cottages now stand, a somewhat
broad and deep ditch ran, or rather crept, its muddy
way along; and skirting this, at some twenty or thirty
yards backwards from the road, stood a range of old
farm buildings, consisting of barns, stables, sheds, etc.;
indeed a portion of them are there still. The opposite,
or left-hand side of the road, (entering the city) and
with which I have more particularly to do, remains
at the present day much as it did years ago : the same
rows of old and of more modernly-erected cottages,
presenting nearly the same appearance now as they
did twenty years back ! I shall not, for obvious rea-
sons, point out to the reader the exact cottage, nor
even the precise row to which I shall presently have
to allude.*

Having stated all I deem necessary in this slight
digression, I will now, continuing the narrative, rejoin
my companions, whom, it will be remembered, I left
some two miles short of our journey's end. We had
gone through our dialogue-parts in the " Brigand,"
and had commenced singing the words to the opening
music, namely,
              " Lo ! morn is breaking ! "
when Powell brought us to a sudden stop by exclaim-

---

* Since the above was written, vast improvements have been
effected on the left-hand side of the road also.

ing "Hush! hark!" just in time for us to catch the echo of the Minster clock, the last note of whose deep-toned bell was then dying on the midnight air. "Two o'clock!" Powell continued, "and morning soon *will* be breaking! therefore I for one vote that we have done with singing now, and move homeward a little faster." Powell was at that time very early in his habits, and had for the last hour shown an anxiety "to move homeward a little faster;" and now, followed by us, pressed forward at a rate somewhat more rapid than the steady pace we had hitherto pursued.

Price was the first to break silence, which he did by observing that he "did not believe that it could be anything like so late as two o'clock." Poor Dan, who never let slip an opportunity to engage in an argument, slackened his pace at this, and the disputation ran, for a time, quite in earnest between the two. Price at length appealed to me by inquiring what I thought the time might be? I agreed with him at once by stating my opinion that it could not be so late (or early) as two o'clock. "Oh!" cried Dan, "as for 'the Baron,' if it took him in the head he wouldn't mind swearing that it was not later than ten o'clock last night!"

"Much obliged to you, friend Dan!" I said, "for your good opinion: nevertheless, I should not much like to swear that it was not ten o'clock to-morrow morning, and that this was not sunlight instead of moonlight, shining around us. However," I added, "you, I doubt not, Daniel, have more than one watch about you, and as yonder shines a beautiful moon, you can satisfy us and yourself in an instant."

"Not if I had a hundred watches, and there were as many moons shining overhead," was his response.

" And why not ? " asked Price.

" Because," answered he, " I should rather each enjoyed his own opinion until we come to the Market-place."

He did not himself, I knew at the time, really believe that the morning had so far advanced as he wished us to think it was ; in fact, he had long before wished himself where, under ordinary circumstances, he would have been hours before, viz. in his bed ; and the argument had, I remember, sufficiently damped our spirits to render us each wishful not only to arrive at the Market-hall, but that we were in bed also : but in this we were destined to meet with an impediment of a nature that we had not at all calculated upon.

We were still inviting Powell to back his opinion by having reference to his watch, and had penetrated far into the Above-Eign, when Price next brought us to a stand-still. Not seeing any reason for this abrupt interruption, we looked at him, in order that he might explain the cause : but, merely observing that " we can know, now, what time it is, and that, too, without waiting till we get to the Market-house," he moved forward in advance to where Powell and myself remained. Dan followed him with his gaze, and I, (who was always near-sighted) stood looking inquiringly at him, hoping for an explanation ; but he, holding up his finger to enjoin silence, vouchsafed to give utterance only to the monosyllable " hush ! " The next moment we heard Price asking some one to " please say what hour of the night it was ?" This question, after a brief silence, he repeated ; when, still receiving no answer, he turned and called on us, in a somewhat subdued tone, to join him. Having done so, we found him looking up, with rather an

embarrassed air, at the window of one of the cottages situated on our left, and at the open casement
of which appeared what seemed to us all to be the
figure of a woman, standing, or rather leaning half
thereout, and apparently gazing at the moon.

We stood looking on in silence for a moment or
two, when I ventured to suggest that "probably she
was asleep." "Asleep! dead, I should say!" rejoined
Price.

Powell, who had not as yet spoken, now directed
his deep, sonorous voice towards the strange object,
by repeating the question before asked by Price. Still
receiving no response, either by word or movement,
I,—stepping somewhat forward,—enquired if "any
one was ill in the room? This attempt proving
equally as futile as the preceding ones, my companions adopted another plan,—that of projecting small
pebbles against the closed half of the casement; and
yet, (although I was fearful lest we should disturb
the neighbours,) it had no more effect than if they
had thrown feathers thereat.

We now desisted for a while, and went forward up
upon the causeway, so as to have a nearer view of
what we (as may be imagined,) had begun to consi-
der as a rather mysterious object. But the closer
inspection we thus obtained was far from clearing up
the mystery, inasmuch as, from what portion of the
figure was revealed to our view, it seemed to us to be
that of a woman attired in the quaint garb most in
vogue about the middle of the last century! The
cloak, or mantle, in which the figure was enwrapped,
appeared to us to be in colour a silvery grey, the hood
of which seemed to be lined with silk or satin of a
somewhat darker shade. On its head it wore one of

those strange-looking bonnets, black in colour, and peculiar in shape to the above-mentioned period—the hind part being fashioned nearly the same as the front—*two pokes* in fact. Beneath this shone a cap of snowy whiteness ; the back part of which (from the position in which the figure stood) alone presented itself to our view.

The attitude was as follows :—The Apparition stood, as it appeared to us, on the floor of the room, its elbow resting on the window-sill ; one side of the face reclining on the palm of the hand, and the face turned (as before observed) upwards, as though gazing at the moon.

During the time we were engaged thus in our nearer inspection, we each of us in turn addressed ourselves to the mysterious object above, in order, if possible, to attract its attention, but all to no purpose, as neither sound nor motion rewarded our united efforts.

We next passed over to the opposite side of the road, in the hope that we should thus gain a view of the features ! but as the road on the ditch-side was, at that time, considerably lower than on the cottage side, we failed in our object. Powell, who was much taller than Price or myself, told us that he fancied he could see the lower part of the face ; and added that, if so, the under-jaw seemed to him to be *dropped*, similar to that of a corpse !

I can scarcely describe what our feelings were at the time ! To say that we experienced no fear, would, perhaps, be wrong ; but certainly it was not sufficiently powerful to conquer our curiosity, which, instead of diminishing, grew stronger every moment.

Our next move was to skirt the ditch for a space,

back the way we had come—turning our gaze back-
ward from time to time, to note if any corresponding
movement had taken place on the part of the extra-
ordinary object that had so strangely attracted our
attention. Nothing transpiring, we again turned
back, down the middle of the road, and came once
more abreast of the cottage, but only to find matters
exactly as we had left them—the casement still open,
and the figure yet there.—We renewed our enquiries
as to "what time of the night it was?" and "if
anyone was ill there?" but with just the same result
as before—the apparition remaining as immovable
as though carved in stone.

Growing more and more interested every moment,
we were again about to try what effect a few more
pebbles would have. For this purpose Powell and
myself were in the act of groping for some, when we
were startled by hearing a deep, rumbling sound in
the room overhead! We turned quickly round, and
seeing Price looking upwards with a somewhat be-
wildered air, we hurriedly inquired the cause. He
made no answer, but continued looking up at the
window until we had repeated the question more than
once. At length he said, " I cast a stone as large as
my fist in at that window, and I could almost swear,"
he added, pointing upwards, "that it went through
that figure likewise."

Having nothing to say in contradiction to this, we
stood silently gazing alternately at each other, and
at the mysterious object above.

I hardly know what impulse could have prompted
us to do so, but we were each of us again stooping
for pebbles, when a low, hollow moan, as of one in
intense pain, struck upon our ear! I remember that

our first hurried glance was cast round towards the opposite side of the road,—as the sound seemed to us to come from that side, rather than from the cottages. Seeing nothing there, I ventured to hint that, perhaps, the moan was uttered by a sleeping horse!—Price shook his head doubtingly at this, whilst Powell declared that he " had never heard such a sound from a horse in his life;"—saying which, he turned again towards the window. He had scarcely done so, when we heard him exclaim, in a voice husky with horror, " Look ! great heaven ! look there !"

We turned quickly round, just in time to see withdrawn from the open casement, and from directly over the figure of the woman, what to us seemed to be the head of a *large white dog !!* This had no sooner disappeared than we were almost stunned by the outburst of a shriek which rose, loud, wild, and unearthly on the calm, midnight air ! Indeed, so full was the sound that it was impossible to tell from whence it came ; and, truth to say, we did not stop to ascertain whether it came from the right hand or the left,—from above or from below ! for a very short space of time found us standing. leaning for support on each other's shoulders, panting for breath. and perspiring at every pore, at least a hundred and fifty yards nearer to the town.

Powell was the first to recover himself, when looking at me he said, " I suppose, friend 'baron,' you will think *that* was a moan from a sleeping horse !" I made no reply to this, but seeing my companions gazing back at the cottages, I enquired if " the woman was still at the window ?"

" She is still there, Tom," said Price.

" And the neighbours ? " I asked, feeling assured

that that awful shriek must have aroused the sleeping denizens of the place.

"There is not a soul or a body else to be seen," was his answer.

"By my soul!" exclaimed Powell in his usually-earnest tone, "if I do not think we are all three be-witched! For my part, stay who will, *I* shall stay no longer!" And, suiting the action to the word, he strode onward, followed by us, towards the turnpike, which at that time stood nearer to the city than now.

The clocks, just at that moment, rang out clear and *unmistakably*, the hour of "two!" but we heeded not the time—cared not who was right or who was wrong! indeed, so engrossed were our mental faculties with the mysteries we had just seen and heard, that the old dispute was not even alluded to.

We soon found ourselves in the centre of our then "dull town," where we parted with each other, and (I can answer for my two friends, no doubt, as I can for myself,) each was not long before he was in bed.

In the morning, as soon as breakfast was over, I proceeded to put in execution a plan I had formed in my own mind during the few hours I had lain in bed. Not feeling satisfied with the termination our adventure had come to in the night, I had determined to revisit the locality in the broad light of day, and to enter upon the scene exactly as myself and friends had come upon it the night before. To effect this, it was necessary that I should take a circuitous route, and this I accomplished by passing up the Barton, along Whitehorse-lane, and so out into the Above Eign. I soon came within view of the cottage, the window of which I saw was still open, but without the strange figure we had seen there the night before.

Almost expecting, to see the apparition make its appearance, I kept my gaze steadily fixed upon the casement; and, as I drew near, I came to the conclusion that the best plan I could adopt was to knock at the door, offer some kind of apology for the midnight rudeness of myself and companions, and trust for a solution of the strange affair to what might occur therefrom. For this purpose I removed my gaze from the window above, and was turning towards the door, when, if I had been astonished the night before, I was now thoroughly thunderstruck, on discovering that the house was—*void!!*

Yes,—the closed shutters, together with the neglected state of the door-step, proclaimed this fact, which had (from the houses being all closed alike during sleeping hours), escaped the notice of myself and friends when we were there the night before.

I have little more to add :—merely to state that, on making this new, and anything but satisfactory discovery, I passed on into the town, feeling that I had taken nothing by my morning's movement, and that I was as far off as ever from solving the mystery of THE SPECTRE OF THE ABOVE EIGN.

———————

NOTE.

IT will be remembered by many of my local readers that about the time to which I refer, certain miscreants were "making night hideous," by plying, in several of our city graveyards, (one of which was situated nearly opposite the back of the cottages to which I allude), their disgusting occupation of "body-snatching!" Whether any of these wretches had, or had not, any thing to do with the matter described in the present sheets, is, of course, more than I can tell—I merely make the suggestion, and will leave the reader to come to what conclusion he may deem a fitting one,

THE END.

www.ingramcontent.com/pod-product-compliance
Lightning Source LLC
Chambersburg PA
CBHW031452270326
41930CB00007B/964